THE
Archive Photographs
SERIES
BUDLEIGH SALTERTON
AND RALEIGH COUNTRY

SIR WALTER RALEIGH

Born at
Hayes Barton
Devon
1552

Died at
Whitehall
London.
1618

Sir Walter Raleigh was born at Hayes Barton, East Budleigh, in 1552 and, despite growing up to become a giant among the giants of the Elizabethan age and travelling throughout the world, his heart always remained among the fields of his Devonshire home. We have his word for it: in later years he wrote to Mr Duke, the owner of his Hayes Barton birthplace, seeking to buy Hayes Barton. 'I am willing to give you whatsoever in your conscience you deem it worth. For having been born in that house I would rather seat myself there than anywhere else.' Sadly his plea fell on deaf ears.

THE
Archive Photographs
SERIES
BUDLEIGH SALTERTON
AND RALEIGH COUNTRY

Compiled by
Les Berry and Gerald Gosling

CHALFORD

First published 1998
Copyright © Les Berry and Gerald Gosling, 1998

The Chalford Publishing Company
St Mary's Mill, Chalford,
Stroud, Gloucestershire, GL6 8NX

ISBN 0 7524 1125 X

Typesetting and origination by
The Chalford Publishing Company
Printed in Great Britain by
Bailey Print, Dursley, Gloucestershire

Contents

Hayes Barton, Sir Walter Ralegh's Coat-of-firms in Birthroom Window. (born 1552, died 1618).

Copyright.

The room in which Sir Walter Raleigh was born at Hayes Barton.

Guess which is me at Budleigh Salterton.

Introduction

It is strange that one of England's greatest explorers and its greatest soldier were born within a few miles of one another in tiny villages in beautiful surroundings in East Devon. John Churchill, later, as the Duke of Marlborough, the thorn in the flesh of Louis XIV and his armies and allies, was born at Ash in Musbury in 1650. His was a glorious career that not even the machinations of politicians in his later years could hide.

Just under a century earlier, some twenty miles away at Hayes Barton in East Budleigh, Walter Raleigh first drew breath in 1552. The most unkindest of cuts was when the trumped-up charges against him included dealing with the Spanish enemy that he had detested all his life.

Stout-hearted Devonian that he was, Raleigh went to the block like a man. No begging for mercy here. A simple request for a pipe of baccy to steady his nerves and he went to meet his maker with a smile.

If, as we are told, a man's life flashes before him during his last moments, Raleigh's would have dwelt with some pleasure on his earlier years as a boy at East Budleigh and the beautiful countryside that he knew so well.

It is still beautiful. The River Otter meanders gently to the sea on the last leg of a journey that started on the Devon-Somerset boundary. It flows through fields and woods and villages and hamlets that have stood in the same places since before Domesday. To the south is the watering place of Budleigh Salterton where, if you believe Millais, the young Walter was wont to go and listen to old salts swopping yarns of derring-do on the high seas and the Spanish Main.

Budleigh has many faces. Once the butt of comic hall jokes, it is an attractive little town with an air of genteel respectability that not even its posh neighbour Sidmouth can match. It does not try to rival the brashness of nearby Exmouth; it does not pretend to be something above its station in life. It is, in fact, a nice place to live in or visit.

Les Berry and Gerald Gosling have given us some fascinating glimpses of the yesteryears of 'Raleigh Country' and its people. They are to be commended for their efforts and I am sure that both locals and visitors will enjoy reading their book.

Tony Gooding,
Budleigh Salterton, 1998

One
East Budleigh
and Bicton

East Budleigh, c. 1910.

The Post Office and Village Stores, East Budleigh, *c.* 1925. Today's post office (seen below in the 1950s) is a few hundred yards down the road. The older post office, latterly tea rooms, has recently been converted into a private house.

East Budleigh, *c.* 1925. The village post office was, for a short spell, situated at premises further down High Street than the original building seen opposite.

All Saints' church at East Budleigh, *c.* 1910. The church dates back to Saxon times, pieces of Saxon work having been found embedded in the walls during restoration work. Most of the present building, however, dates from the fifteenth century. The peal of bells was increased to eight when two treble bells from the closed St John's church in Devonport were recast and brought to East Budleigh.

Holly Tree Cottage, East Budleigh, *c.* 1899.

Despite being the birthplace of one of England's best-known heroes, East Budleigh never cashes in on the tourist trade in the manner that towns and villages with more tenuous claims to fame often do. Instead it remains essentially a working Devonshire farm village, as in this view looking down the High Street in the 1920s, and is none the worse for that.

The Octagon, a tiny building in East Budleigh's High Street, seen above in around 1910, was once actually lived in, but it fell into disrepair and was demolished around 1970.

The bridge and stream, with All Saints' church peeping out over the cottages in the background, in the late 1890s.

Wynards Farm, East Budleigh, opposite the village school, was burnt down before the First World War.

Hayes Barton, near East Budleigh, c. 1910. Raleigh's birthplace is E-shaped, a compliment to the Queen which is a feature of many Elizabethan houses.

The kitchen at Hayes Barton in the 1920s.

East Budleigh station, c. 1913. Although most visitors think it is Otterton station, being just a few yards from the village, it is in fact in East Budleigh parish and takes its name from there.

East Budleigh station, *c.* 1960.

East Budleigh station (*c.* 1960) was built in 1897 and opened, along with the rest of the branch line to Budleigh Salterton, on 15 May that year.

East Budleigh School, c. 1964. It is said that there was a school in the village as early as 1705, and by 1820 the master was paid £32; his duties included running a Sunday class for those unable to attend during the week because of work.

East Budleigh football team, 1955-56, when the side won the Exeter & District League Junior One championship and the Football Express and Golesworthy Cups. The club was formed in 1926-27, competing in the now defunct Ottery & District League and the Golesworthy Cup, winning both at the first attempt. For some seasons now the first team has been competing successfully in senior football. The team here is, back row, left to right: Frank Mitchell, Cyril Hayman (chairman), Arthur Skinner, Monty Elliott, Syd Skinner, Ken Luxton, Bob Brownhill (who scored 77 goals that season), Gerald Troake, Arthur Pratt (treasurer), Bob Murdock (linesman). Front: Percy Pinney, Peter Dunster, Robert Pratt (capt), Les Williams, Mike Board.

When Bicton College of Agriculture, East Budleigh, was established in 1947 as the Devon Farm Institute, it had twenty students and nine staff. Today the College has 800 full-time students studying on courses from introductory level to Higher National Diploma. In addition approximately 2,000 students come to Bicton to study on a part-time basis. This aerial picture of the College in 1976 is of considerable interest as it shows the old tennis court and car park in the rear which are now part of the site of the Halls of Residence.

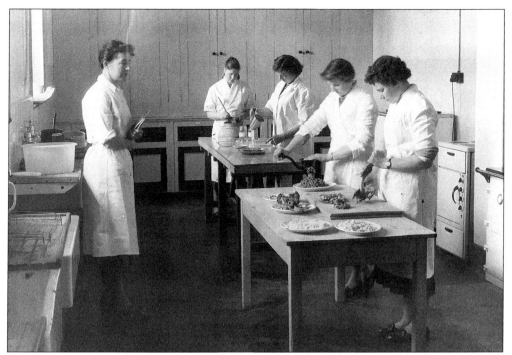

Lesley Roden at the Devon Farm Institute, Bicton, with students taking the full-time Agricultural Course For Women, which included Home Economics.

Alan Pring keeps a close eye on the furrows during a ploughing match at Bicton College of Agriculture, c. 1957.

The Flint Lodge, Bicton, *c.* 1909. It has since been demolished and replaced by a modern building.

Tower and Green Drive in Baker's Brake, Bicton, *c.* 1840. The large China Tower was a gift from Lady Rolle to her husband when he was recovering from a long illness. It took two footmen to carry him to the top of the winding staircase in a specially designed chair. They had to struggle up 120 stairs so that he could enjoy the view.

Bicton House in 1907, covered in scaffolding during restoration work.

Bicton House from a painting by G.B. Campion of 1831 which he 'respectfully inscribes to the Right Honourable Lord Rolle'. The gardens are laid out in the Italian style by Henry (later Lord) Rolle to designs by André le Notre. The famous arboretum was planted in 1830 and its trees and shrubs from all over the world have attracted thousands of people down the years.

RULES of BICTON

		d.
1.	Coming to work on a Monday morning with a dirty shirt	3
2.	Coming to work any morning without shoes being laced or tied	3
3.	Any person employed in these departments found gathering fruit with unwashed hands	4
4.	Going into any hothouse, greenhouse, &c., or walking on any gravel walk, with dirty shoes	3
5.	Taking a wheelbarrow with a dirty wheel on the walks, or in any other way making dirt and not immediately cleaning the same up	3
6.	Leaving any door or gate open in any department of the garden	3
7.	Leaving any door or gate unlocked, after opening the same, and not returning the key to its proper place	3
8.	Leaving any stoke-hole dirty, not keeping the ashes cleaned out from under the grate, not sifting the cinders once a week	3
9.	Leaving any fire at night not in proper trim or order	3
10.	Leaving any thing dangerous in or about the stokeholes or furnaces	12
11.	Leaving a job unfinished, in an unworkmanlike manner	3
12.	Making any waste of coals, dropping them about, or not keeping them swept clean up together	3
13.	Leaving open the cover of any boiler or cistern	6
14.	Smoking a pipe of tobacco in the hours of work	4
15.	Neglecting to grease a wheelbarrow when requisite	3
16.	Leaving any tool, wheelbarrow, steps, ladder, water-pot, &c., out of its proper place, or putting it away dirty	3
17.	Leaving rubbish in any hothouse or greenhouse, or in any way making dirty and not immediately cleaning the same up	3
18.	Leaving heaps of grass, weeds, leaves, or any rubbish whatever, about the pleasure-grounds, borders, walks, &c., for each heap	3
19.	Carelessly breaking any plant, pan, glass, tool, &c.	3
20.	Breaking any flower-pot with plants in it, and not immediately potting the same plants properly	6
21.	Neglecting to do a job after having been once told of it	3
	the second time	6
22.	Neglecting to attend to water fountains, &c.	3
23.	Any man found at his work intoxicated shall forfeit his day's wages, and be otherwise dealt with as thereafter shall be considered just	
24.	Swearing or making use of bad language, for every separate evil expression	3
25.	Damaging or in any way mutilating or defacing the above Rules	12

The Bicton Rules. One doubts whether they would be popular with the students of today's College of Agriculture.

The Kings Arms, East Budleigh, *c.* 1925.

East Budleigh, *c.* 1906. There is a school of thought that attributes the Budleigh part of the name to the Old English 'budda', or beetle, used as a personal name. It is called 'Bodlelia' in Domesday and appears in many forms in old documents, including 'Boddelegh', 'Boddeleghe', 'Budelega' and 'Buteleg' among others.

The Rolle Arms, East Budleigh, *c.* 1908, when Izaac Richards was the licensee.

The Rolle Arms, East Budleigh, *c.* 1905.

Two
Budleigh Salterton
The Town

The old limekilns at Budleigh Salterton from a pencil drawing in 1837. Long since fallen into disrepair, they went when the entrance to the car park was improved and changed to one-way.

Budleigh Salterton Fire Brigade on the Green in around 1900. The men are too well dressed to be heading to or from a fire, especially the driver with his hat.

Budleigh Salterton National Fire Service, 1944. The group includes men from surrounding villages. Back row, left to right: Firemen S. Elliot, E. Hellier, E. Prew, A. Hitt, A. Mitchell, P. Paver, C. Gooding, W. Wright, P. Eaton, F. Letton, R. Clemens. Second row: Firemen E. Board, H. Perkins, J. Patch, F. Avery, C. Till, H. Tully, S. Heard, F. Knight, F. Stuart, H. Stapleton, R. Bastone. Third row: Firemen J. Ware, C. Jewell, H. Yates, J. Harris, E. Prew, F. Dunscombe, W. Harding, W. Pearcey, T. Sparkes, M. Sellek, H. Staddon. S. Gooding. Front row: Firemen C. Smale, E. Sellek, F. Sedgemore, Leading Firemen W. Searle, T. Sedgemore, Company Officer J.B. Holden, Leading Fireman P. Potier, F. Cole, H. Carter, A. Noon.

Budleigh Salterton's former fire engine, which was pensioned off and now forms part of a private collection at Cullompton.

An early Blackburn postcard from around the turn of the century showing a donkey cart in what most people agree is Moor Lane. F.T. Blackburn was probably the town's leading photographer in Edwardian days, working from his studio in Station Road and show rooms at 17 High Street.

The Otterton–Exmouth bus. One school of thought claims it was run by Mr Hart, who ran a garage at Clinton Terrace in Budleigh Salterton; others feel the bus, seen here in the 1920s, predates that.

F.T. Blackburn was probably the town's best-known family photographer in late Victorian and Edwardian Budleigh Salterton. He was particularly well known for his local views, which were in great demand, especially by guidebooks of the time like *Mate's Illustrated Budleigh Salterton*, the local version of a popular guide produced by the Bournemouth printers W. Mate & Son. Blackburn claimed that his 'photographs of children were specially taken by a new instantaneous process' and that his 'enlargements were a success'. He also 'supplied amateurs'.

Probably the best known painting by John Everett Millais (1829-96), one of the founders of the Pre-Raphaelite Movement, was 'The Boyhood of Raleigh'. It shows the explorer as a youth on Budleigh Salterton beach spellbound at the feet of a mariner telling tales of high adventure on the high seas. The other boy is said to be his kinsman Humphrey Gilbert. The wall behind the two boys still stands on the Promenade (below).

MILLAIS' HOUSE AND RALEIGH'S WALL BUDLEIGH SALTERTON   KU393

Harvesting on Otter Head in the 1920s. Of particular interest is the seldom-seen view of the final meanderings of the River Otter as it reaches the sea after a long journey which began in the high and lonely Blackdown Hills on the Devon-Somerset border.

The Granary, Budleigh Salterton, c. 1910. The small buildings in front of the granary were the 'bottom-of-the-garden' toilets of the neighbouring cottages. Although these and the house behind the granary have been demolished the granary remains, recently converted to a handsome split-level house.

RIVER OTTER. SOUTH BRIDGE. NEAR BUDLEIGH SALTERTON.

The old wooden South Bridge over the River Otter, seen here during the Second World War, was replaced around the 1960s by a more modern concrete bridge that will take loads up to 32 tons.

BUDLEIGH-SALTERTON _ From the Sea.

A sketch of Budleigh Salterton in the mid-nineteenth century shows how late the town's development as a watering place, accelerated by the arrival of the railway, really was.

The existence of Donkeys' Turn (seen in the background), along which donkeys carrying seaweed from the rocks at Ottermouth and locally caught fish and crabs were led, was recently questioned by East Devon District Council when Budleigh Salterton Town Council wanted it restored after erosion protection works had been carried out in the area. The path leading to Donkey's Turn was washed away in the early 1970s. The bottom picture (*c.* 1907) shows the view from Otter Head looking back towards the town.

The Parade, Budleigh Salterton, *c.* 1904.

The Parade, Budleigh Salterton, looking west in 1902. The steamer in the background is probably the *Duchess of Devonshire*, which plied along the coastal resorts between Plymouth and Bournemouth. It was a 230-ton ship owned by the South Devon & West Bay Steamship Company and was sold for scrap after running aground at Sidmouth on 27 August 1934.

The beach at Budleigh Salterton with the Parade around 1895. The coastguard station, with its cottages behind, is on the top of the hill. It is interesting to note how much lower the shingle was then that it is today. This picture, like the one below showing the view looking back into the town, was the work of W.B. Wells, who, as well as being a photographer, ran a Fancy Bazaar in the town.

The Beach and Parade, Budleigh Salterton, *c.* 1880. Budleigh Brook at this time ran directly into the sea. By the time of the lower picture (probably just after the turn of the century) shingle blocked the mouth and the brook had to drain through it to reach the sea. Today the bridge has gone and this part of the brook has been piped and culverted.

35

Looking from the Cliff Path to Exmouth towards Budleigh Salterton beach in around 1910. Guests at the Rosemullion Hotel made frequent use of this path to reach the beach.

The West End Slopes, Budleigh Salterton, in around 1899. In later years steps were built on the path to make it easier for passengers to walk down to the beach for a trip on the paddle steamers that called at Budleigh. The steps, known for obvious reasons as the Steamers Steps, are still there.

Budleigh Salterton in around 1905. The *Duchess of Devonshire* steamer called three or four times a week in the season, sailing times being well advertised in the town. At ports of call without a pier, such as Budleigh Salterton, an unusual but simple method of taking on and discharging passengers was used: a flying bridge was placed from the bow to the shore, as seen in the picture above.

Jim and Dinah Perriam paddle beside the *Duchess* in the very early 1930s.

The Steamers Steps and West End Slopes, Budleigh Salterton, *c.* 1920.

Budleigh's beach was festooned with barbed wire and piping in 1940 when the threat of invasion was very real. No doubt the piping would have been effective in (temporarily) stopping tanks driving into Budleigh. In the absence of any German invaders, its most popular use was to provide play areas for small (and not so small) boys!

The roads leading from the beach were also partially blocked with concrete tank traps. Such defences were not supposed to be photographed: the German Fifth Column was dropping everywhere by parachute, disguised as nuns if you listened to paranoid officialdom! The type of concrete constructions seen above towards New Road had proved quite effective against tanks in the Maginot Line (until the Germans simply drove around them) and there was no reason to suppose they would have been anything but effective if the Germans had arrived at Budleigh Salterton. Those seen below blocked the entrance to Fore Street at the Round Corner.

The Round Corner, Budleigh Salterton, *c.* 1935.

The Octagon, on the corner of Fore Street and Marine Parade, Budleigh Salterton, *c.* 1937. This was once the home of Millais and he painted his famous 'Boyhood of Raleigh' here.

Fore Street, Budleigh Salterton, *c.* 1919.

Fore Street, Budleigh Salterton, *c.* 1902. At one time there were eight businesses in the town belonging to different members of the Cowd family. William Cowd owned the millinery and clothing shop on the extreme right which traded as Cowd & Son. There was no son, however. His daughter Zilliah later changed the business into an antique shop. Three doors nearer (out of sight in this view) was Sydney Cowd's grocery shop.

Fore Street, Budleigh Salterton, *c.* 1907.

Fore Street, Budleigh Salterton, *c.* 1908. Many of the buildings on the immediate right have since been replaced.

The drapery business of M. Gush & Son, seen here in 1902, occupied three blocks (Nos 6, 7 and 8) in Budleigh Salterton High Street.

Fore Street, 1932. This postcard was sent to a Mr Hicks at Ashburton by someone called Hilda who was staying at 27 Fore Street. She writes that she 'finds the people nice and friendly and everyone is trying to make us feel at home ... is quite pleased with the shops and everything is in perfect order.'

Fore Street, *c.* 1955. Davie & Son's greengrocers shop on the left is now Prior's Upholstery and carpet shop.

Fore Street, *c.* 1895.

The Library, Fore Street, seen above in 1928, was owned by Frank Parsons. At the time of the lower picture (1902), when the business had been established in the town for over a century, he advertised that he was the publisher of the Budleigh Salterton railway timetable and the Visitors' List. He also issued tickets for Bicton Gardens and gave information on the Lawn Tennis & Croquet Club, the Cricket Club and the Hockey Club. He was also the agent for several newspapers, ran a printing works, sold golf clubs, was a Sun Fire and Life agent and a photographer, and framing pictures was a speciality.

Rolle Square, Budleigh Salterton, seen here in around 1909, took its name from the Rolle Hotel (out of sight on the immediate left). Fore Street ended here, High Street taking the traffic on towards Exmouth. The handsome building on the right, on the corner of High Street and Chapel Street, was the local branch of the Devon & Cornwall bank. Later (below) it became Wilson's Grocery Stores.

G. Bennett, whose High Street shop is seen here in 1902, was a man with many irons in the fire. Besides being a furnisher, he was an ironmonger, a builder and decorator, and a house agent. He also advertised as a plumber, gas fitter, hot water and sanitary engineer, a wire and electric bell fitter and a range and grate fitter. He found time to stock guns, rifles, ammunition, bedding and bedsteads, linoleums, oilcloths, mattings, mats, river and sea fishing tackle, tennis and gold requisites, and bathing and other tents. And, if you asked, he could probably supply the proverbial kitchen sink!

Harry Perriam's grocery business was among Budleigh Salterton's oldest established family businesses having been in the town since 1812. He was also a wine and beer merchant. In this picture, which dates from around 1903, the staff are posing outside the shop in High Street. Of particular interest is the errand boy to the left with his delivery barrow, a forerunner of the errand boy's bike. Perriam's telephone number was a magnificent Budleigh Salterton 3.

High Street, *c.* 1922.

Henry Pillar was established at 14 High Street as a watchmaker, silversmith and optician.

The Feathers Hotel, Budleigh Salterton. In 1901, at that time of the top picture, the hotel was owned by Harry Worth, who, like many hoteliers of the time, hired out carriages, waggonettes, brakes and dog carts from his stables. In the 1960s (below) the Feathers was still one of Budleigh's more popular pubs, although by then the landlord had stopped leaving his coach and pair on the yellow lines.

Hooper's Stores, High Street, c. 1961. Then a grocers and off-licence, today this is a branch of Threshers.

The post office, High Street, c. 1909. Although the sorting office is retained at the rear of this building and larger parcels are still accepted here, the day-to-day business of a modern post office is now conducted from a newsagents in High Street.

Mr H. Bickley was a butcher in High Street in 1902. He advertised himself as 'a purveyor of choice English Meat', whose 'pickled silversides, briskets and Ox Tongues were always ready'. Mr A.H. Webber (below), another of the town's butchers, could be found at 42 High Street. He also advertised his Pickled Ox Tongues, etc., and went on to claim that he sold 'the very best Ox and Heifer Beef, Wether Mutton, Veal, Lamb and Dairy-fed Pork'.

The Rolle Hotel, Budleigh Salterton, 1902, when it was under the management of Miss G.H. Holman, who had previously held a similar post at the Union Hotel in Penzance. The lawn facing the sea was large enough for two tennis courts or a bowling green and croquet lawn. The hotel ran a conveyance between Budleigh and Exmouth four times a week during the summer months and also met all trains with its own bus. It had a particularly sporting flavour. Fishing tickets for the Otter could be obtained here, and special terms were available for 'Ladies and Gentlemen attending the magnificent Golf Links'.

The front of the Rolle Hotel facing Fore Street in around 1910.

Aerial view of Budleigh Salterton in the late 1930s. The Rolle Hotel, seen in the centre of the picture, was demolished around the 1970s, virtually leaving the town without a hotel.

F.G. Gregory was a Family Grocer and Provision Merchant at 10 High Street at the turn of the century. By a coincidence his telephone number was also 10. He was an agent for the Heavitree Brewery and Carpenter & Co.'s ales and stouts.

St Peter's church, opposite The Lawn and below West Terrace, in 1902. Designed by Mr G.H. Fellowes Prynne, and built by Luscombe & Son of Exeter in just under two years from the date of the first stone's being laid by Miss M. Rolle on 24 November 1891, St Peter's was consecrated by the Bishop of Exeter on 25 April 1893. It replaced the old Rolle Chapel and had room for as many as 800 worshippers. In 1942 serious damage was caused when a bomb hit the north side of the church. The nearby Assembly Rooms were also damaged. Restoration work was completed in 1952.

Budleigh Salterton, St. Peter's Church.

Westbourne Terrace, West Hill, *c.* 1906. The area behind the two boys has been developed.

Jean's Cottage, Rolle Road, in the 1930s. Formerly part of a block of fishermen's cottages, it was the popular port of call at the time. It is now a restaurant known as Thorney's.

Sherbrooke Chine, Budleigh Salterton, 1908. The steps connected the East Devon Golf Club with the beach. During the Second World War, when the Chine would have made a good path inland for invaders, it was blocked with barbed wire and mined.

West Hill, looking into Fountain Hill and North View Road (on the left), *c.* 1900. The horse trough is still there but is now part of the town's floral display.

Links Road, *c.* 1912. The empty spaces on both sides of the immediate foreground have been built on.

East Terrace, *c.* 1912. These handsome buildings happily remain with us, although the right hand one has been recently restored.

Victoria Place, *c.* 1910.

Cliff Terrace, *c.* 1920.

Station Road, *c.* 1910. The field behind the fence on the right is now The Green. In the picture below, showing the town (bottom) end of Station Road, the Gospel Hall can be seen on the right. It closed in 1997.

Budleigh Salterton station, *c.* 1959. The branch line from Tipton St John on the Sidmouth line was opened on 15 May 1897 and extended to Exmouth six years later. It was taken over by the Southern Railway in 1923 and became part of Britsh Rail in 1948. Diesel replaced steam in 1963 but the line was closed to paasengers in 1967 and the track removed soon after. The entire station was demolished and flats known as Stanley Mews were erected on part of the site; they are named after station master Stanley Murch. The rest of the site was taken over by Normans, the cash-and-carry stores.

Budleigh Salterton station in the 1950s.

The passengers' footbridge at Budleigh Salterton station in around 1959.

The Rosemullion Hotel in the 1930s, when it faced the sea. All but the left hand wing of what was once the town's leading hotel has been demolished and replaced by flats.

John Palmer, a Budleigh Salterton builder and decorator in the 1920s, had a shop at 32 High Street.

Fore Street decorated for the Silver Jubilee of King George V in 1935.

Knowle Hill, *c.* 1900.

Little Knowle Road, *c.* 1910.

Little Knowle, *c.* 1903.

Knowle Village, *c.* 1905. The thatched building on the right was the Dog and Donkey Inn. Now rebuilt and renamed the Britannia Inn, it contains a fine matchstick model of the original building.

Knowle Village, *c.* 1908. The buildings on the left vanished in post-Second World War road-widening schemes.

Knowle Hill in the 1930s. This junction, where the road forked for Exmouth or Exeter, is built virtually over the Exmouth branch line. It has been improved in recent years by conversion to a roundabout.

Three
Budleigh Salterton
The People

The East Devon Hunt meet at Black Hill in around 1919.

A street party to celebrate Queen Victoria's Diamond Jubilee outside Perriam's grocery shop in Budleigh Salterton's High Street in 1897.

The same party, but this time looking the other way.

An outing to a now unknown destination poses outside Kelland's shop in around 1905.

Spectators below the coastguard station watching Budleigh Salterton Regatta before the First World War. The flag in the background belongs to the Budleigh Salterton Swimming and Life Saving Club.

Walking entries in Budleigh Salterton's 1910 Carnival.

Budleigh Salterton cubs at camp at Lympstone, *c.* 1937.

The First Budleigh Salterton scout troop in winter camp at Gilwell Park in 1950.

Members of the First Budleigh Salterton scout troop planning a hike on the bonnet of a Standard 8 Tourer in around 1956.

Budleigh Salterton High Street awash with flags and bunting for an Empire Day in the 1930s.

Budleigh residents enjoy a tea party for either the Silver Jubilee of George V in 1935 or the coronation of George VI in 1937.

The celebrations for the Silver Jubilee of King George V and Queen Mary on 6 May 1935 began in Budleigh Salterton with an Assembly of Public Bodies on the sea front, followed by a procession to Station Road, headed by the British Legion Band. At Station Road a Thanksgiving Service was held in the car park. In the afternoon the Children's Fancy Dress Carnival and Procession marched to the football field. Tea was served to the children (adults were charged 6d) and Jubilee mugs were distributed. In the evening the festivities continued with sports, a whist drive, a dance, and a bonfire on the Jubilee Field.

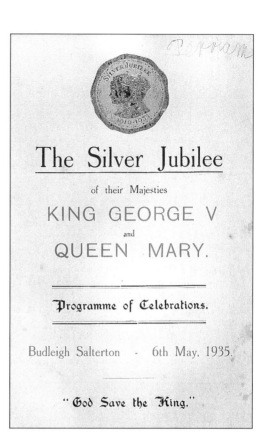

The Silver Jubilee

of their Majesties

KING GEORGE V

and

QUEEN MARY.

Programme of Celebrations.

Budleigh Salterton - 6th May, 1935.

" God Save the King."

THE CORONATION

of their Majesties

KING GEORGE VI

and

QUEEN ELIZABETH

Programme of Celebrations.

Budleigh Salterton - 12th May, 1937.

" God Save the King."

Two years later, on 12 May 1937, the coronation of King George VI and Queen Elizabeth was celebrated in Budleigh Salterton in much the same way. This time, however, there was a dinner for all the inhabitants of the town over the age of 16. It was held in the car park in Station Road and two sittings were necessary. The children, who had received their mugs in the morning, had their teas later.

73

Children's Fancy Dress entrants for the 1930 Budleigh Salterton Carnival held on 16 October. The procession formed up at 6.30 in Coastguards Road and marched off at 7 o'clock, travelling through the Parade, Fore Street, High Street and West Street, turning at Links Road and going back through West Hill, Station Road, Moor Lane, and Clinton Terrace to finish at the Town Hall for the final judging.

Mr A.W. Pidsley's Luncheon and Tea Rooms, Fore Street, 1902. The family bakery had been established in the town since 1824 and was especially popular at the time with the visiting trade who could enjoy a sea view with their Devonshire cream teas ... and all with the same 'Hovis Bread as supplied to H.M. The King'.

Thomas Acland Edmonds, vicar of Budleigh Salterton from 1918 to 1947, with his curate, Mr F.R. Moses (right) and verger, Mr Ayres, outside St Peter's church in 1939.

Below: Budleigh Salterton Red Cross outside their headquarters in Meadow Road, c. 1956. Among those present are Sir Treffery Thompson (County Commissioner), centre of middle row, Ann Whitfield, Jenny Hitt, Janet Miller, Wendy Vinnicombe, Margory Down, Rosemary Sansom (all in the front row), Maureen Miller (with flag), Pat Carter, Sue Broomfield Jones, Mrs Snowshaw, Madge Andrews, Miss Lilian Pearsey, and Mrs Gannon. A detachment of the Red Cross was formed in Budleigh Salterton in 1911 to provide nursing support for the local community. It acquired its own premises in Meadow Road, where it continues today. The services provided have changed from purely nursing to meet the changing face of society with more practical help such as transport for the elderly, the loan of a whole range of items from wheelchairs to commodes, and normal First Aid training and duties.

Budleigh Salterton WI Christmas Sale, *c.* 1956. Left to right: Betty Daniel, Mrs Webber, Ruth Roots, -?-.

The opening of Budleigh Salterton Football Club's new clubhouse in 1967 by Mr Harwood-Fryer. Those present include Bob Hill, Graham Gillard, Jim Callender, Pickles Abbot, Terry Paver and Jim Everest.

A golf course was opened at Otterton Park in 1894. It was of nine holes and had a small pavilion. Although well patronised, it ceased to exist once the East Devon Golf Club was established on 31 March 1902. Members are seen above on the opening day. The new course had eighteen holes. There were magnificent views in all directions from the course and the attractive club house (shown below). The new course, the property of Lord Clinton, admitted visitors to the club house and green on payment of two shillings and six pence per day, ten shillings per week, or thirty shillings per month.

The Lawn Tennis and Croquet Club, West Terrace, Budleigh Salterton, seen here in 1901, was founded in around 1850 as the Budleigh Salterton Archery Club. Croquet was added twenty years later and tennis followed soon afterwards. By the turn of the century the archery section had been relegated to a small adjoining field, and by the time of this picture had ceased altogether.

Budleigh Salterton Lawn Tennis and Croquet Club's team and the London team in 1958. Back row, left to right: C.V. West (Groundsman), J.W. Solomon (London), Major G.F. Stone (Budleigh Salterton), R.F. Rothwell (L), A.J. Cooper (BS), J.G. Warwick (BS), W.P. Omerod (BS). Middle row: J.A. Holliweg (L), Ian Baillieu (L), Miss E.J. Warwick (BS), Lt-Col. G.E. Cave (BS), M.B. Reckitt (L). Front row: Mrs W. Longman (L), W. Longman (L), Mrs E. Rotherham, capt. (BS), E.P.C. Cotter, capt. (L), Col. D.W. Beamish (BS).

Tenants of the Clinton estate at Tidwell House, Budleigh Salterton. Judging by the uniformed lady in the front the picture would appear to have been taken during the Second World War. It is not thought to show a rent day but rather a social occasion of some sort.

Mackerel fishing on Budleigh Salterton beach in 1909. Even at the turn of the century Budleigh fishermen were complaining that fish were becoming scarcer on this part of the coast. They were mainly dependent at the time on herring and mackerel fishing and, to a lesser extent, on crabs and lobsters.

Budleigh residents tuck in during the celebrations for the Diamond Jubilee of Queen Victoria in 1897.

More Diamond Jubilee celebrations. This time the children have been allowed to join in.

An entry for an Edwardian Budleigh Salterton carnival poses outside the Feathers Hotel in High Street.

A Budleigh Salterton Carnival Queen being crowned outside the Public Hall in the 1930s. The Queen, preceded by two heralds and followed by four maids of honour, crossed to the waggon from the hall via a plank.

The 'Uncle Tom Cobley' tableau in a 1930s Budleigh Salterton carnival. During the procession the 'Old Mare' did actually lie down and die and Uncle Tom and his mates all fell on the road.

Four

Otterton

Otterton before 1902. Drakes butchers shop on the left was later pulled down and replaced by Sunnyside. The girl on the bridge is Elizabeth Dowell.

Fore Street, Otterton, 1900. Basclose on the left was built around 1580 and enlarged in 1627 by the Clapp family. The cottages on the right were demolished in 1923 and replaced by the Village Hall.

This is thought to show part of Otterton's celebrations marking the cessation of hostilities in 1918. The tree on the right has been set in the ground as part of the decorations. Mary Ann Baker and her daughter Alice (hatless) stand outside the end cottage, in which they lived.

The Kings Arms, Fore Street, *c.* 1910. The present inn was built in 1889 to replace a building known as the New Inn until 1795, when it changed its name to Kings Arms.

Basclose and Sunnyside Cottages, *c.* 1908. Mrs Ethel Coates (the licensee's wife from the Kings Arms) and Mrs Berry are outside the pub.

Fore Street, *c.* 1911, looking west, with Basclose on the right. Note the monkey puzzle tree.

Fore Street, *c.* 1908, looking east, with the post office in the centre on the right. The cottages on the left were demolished in the 1930s.

The Green, *c.* 1910. These cottages on the north side of the Green were pulled down in 1938.

The Green, *c.* 1907. All the cob and thatch cottages in the terrace on the right have been shops at different times, including a grocers, drapers, shoemakers and newsagents, and even a police house.

The Green, looking north in around 1907. The house on the right may have been the Golden Lion inn, which closed in 1783. The cottages on the left were built in 1874; those in the centre were demolished in 1938.

Bell Street, c. 1910, showing the Northcott family. Crosstrees farmhouse was built in 1876 to replace an earlier building that had been destroyed by fire.

The Smithy, Otterton, seen here in 1907, was in the Northcott family's hands between 1830 and 1929.

Bill Northcott (in the straw boater) with others outside the smithy in 1910.

Otterton post office and shop in 1905, when George Freeman was postmaster.

The post office received a shop extension in 1925, seen here in 1930, by which time Harry Genge, who had been in partnership with George Freeman from 1922 until the latter's death in 1929, was postmaster.

Otterton Garage, seen here in the 1930s, was built on the site of Gosling's Smithy. The manager Frank Cole poses with 'Snapper'.

North Star Farm, Otterton, *c.* 1910. The farm (in the centre background) was later demolished, but North Star Cottage (dated 1689) remains today.

Maunders Hill, c. 1908. Jacketts is the house in the centre, with Conway Cottage beyond it. The cottages on both the right and left were later demolished. Mrs Bolt and Thirsa White pose with Fred and Charlie Snell.

Bell Street, c. 1909. The wall on the left is part of the village pound. Mr Drake's butchers shop on the right was situated in Fore Street until 1902. It had been a smithy owned by one of the Northcott family (see p. 89).

Ottery Street in 1905, looking towards Northcott's smithy. The terraced cottages were built in the 1830s.

Mr W.J. Andrews butchers shop in Otterton in 1938. Frank Payne, the delivery man beside the van, took over the business in 1951.

Constable William Phillips and his wife outside Otterton Police House in 1914. The House, now 9 The Green, was the police house from the 1880s until 1924.

Otterton scout troop in 1927. Back row, left to right: Frank Payne, Frank Smith, Roy Grey, Len Paver, Edgar Paver. Front row: Charlie Paver, Fred Till, Eric Trooke, Harry Pile.

Army recruits prepare to leave Otterton in 1914 for service in Kitchener's Army.

Otterton FC (The Rollers) in 1905. The manager, centre of the back row, is Bill Coate, licensee of the Kings Arms. Among those seen here are Lewis and Frank Burch.

Otterton FC at the opening by George Northcott of the new ground at Stanyway in the 1950s. Back row, left to right: Frank Cole, Peter Elliott, Alan Miller, Malcolm Telford, George Northcott, Monty Elliott, Norman Buckle, Fred Bastin, -?-. Front: Bert Rawlings, Wilf Manns, Mike Dorman, Wilf Pugsley, Keith Prew, Harry Manns.

Otterton Football Club's Stanyway ground was presented to them by George Northcott in the 1950s. He is seen here cutting the tape on Opening Day. Also present are: Major and Mrs Bennett, Frank Cole, Redvers Please, Chris Manns, Michael Dorman, Wilf Manns, Monty Elliott, Norman Buckle, Alan Miller, Mrs Gamble with Elaine Radford and Deirdre Gamble.

Mrs Snell with her son Fred making Honiton lace outside her Conway Cottage home in Otterton's Maunders Hill in around 1910.

A 1925 Otterton WI outing to Weymouth, a long journey when charabancs were limited by law to 12 m.p.h. The ladies, all in their Sunday best hats, are Meggy Till, Alma Till, Polly Paver, Polly Tripe, Frances Vinnicombe, Susan Marks, Fanny Follett, Mrs Pengelly, Bessie Jenner, Louie Follett, Mrs Home, Ruth Baker, Mrs Herbie Baker and Mabel Grey.

Otterton School, *c.* 1914. The teachers are Miss Wakeham and Miss Emily Baker.

A 1929 Otterton School group. Among those seen here are Roy Grey, Reg Wotton, Ralph Eustace, Fred Hitchcock, Charlie Elliott, Frank Payne, Frank Hodge, Frank Smith, Percy Elliott, Fred Till, Amy Marchant, Ernest Payne, Cyril Rice, Edgar Paver, Ivan Paver and Betty Sanders.

Otterton schoolchildren help out with one of the village's many wartime salvage drives in around 1940.

Otterton's 1911 celebrations on the Green for the coronation of King George V. Mabel Prew is standing on the right with Robert and Sarah Carter and their children, Frank, Charlie, Victor and Florence, and their uncle, William Rugg. Among the others about to tuck in are the Pavers, the Smiths, the Vinnicombes, the Burchs, Mr and Mrs Hall, Lilly Chappell and the Revd Seymour, the vicar, who is standing and wearing his clerical hat.

George Northcott in his Naval Artificers uniform during the First World War. The son of Bill Northcott, Otterton's blacksmith, he ran a wallpaper business between the wars and into the 1950s. He moved to Nutwell House, Lympstone, where he continued to be a benefactor of the Northcott Theatre in Exeter.

St Michael's church and the bridge, Otterton, c. 1094. St Michael's was built in 1871 to replace a building dedicated to St Thomas which had in turn replaced an earlier church pulled down at the time of the Dissolution. The earliest mention of the oldest building is 1161.

Ladram Bay, 1840. The arches have since been washed into stacks.

Ladram Bay in 1930. The huts were built to house fishermen's tackle.

Ladram Bay, c. 1904.

The Cottage at Ladram Bay was occupied by the coastguards in the mid-nineteenth century, but by 1910, the time of this picture, it was being used as a tea room. Today it is a private house.

Bicton church, c. 1920.

The Manor House, c. 1905.

Mrs Hitchcock outside her Otterton home in around 1910.

Otterton School, 1907.

Five

Colaton Raleigh and Newton Poppleford

The celebration arch for King George VI's coronation in Hawkerland Road, Colaton Raleigh in 1937.

Colaton Raleigh, *c.* 1914.

Hawkerland church, Colaton Raleigh, at the turn of the century. It was converted into a house in 1970 but the lovely east window was retained. The tiny church had just one bell to which several boys tied a long rope after clambering in through the window. They then went into the field behind the church and kept pulling until William Sellek, the ringer, and several other curious people came to investigate a bell ringing by itself!

Colaton Raleigh, 1932. The two trees, also seen in the picture opposite, are gone today.

Colaton Raleigh, *c.* 1908.

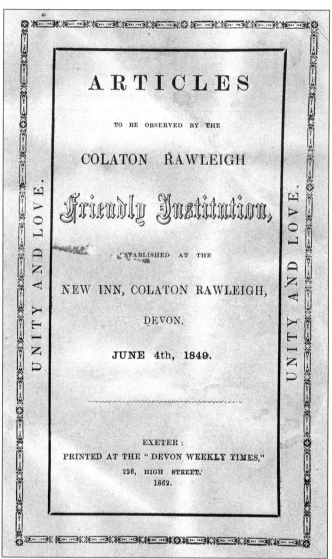

ARTICLES

TO BE OBSERVED BY THE

COLATON RAWLEIGH

Friendly Institution,

ESTABLISHED AT THE

NEW INN, COLATON RAWLEIGH,

DEVON,

JUNE 4th, 1849.

EXETER :
PRINTED AT THE " DEVON WEEKLY TIMES,"
226, HIGH STREET.
1862.

The Colaton Rawleigh (sic) Friendly Society was established at the New Inn in the village on 4 June 1849. It existed to 'establish and maintain a fund for the mutual benefit and support of each other under such calamities as Almighty God may please to inflict upon us'. It met on the first Mondays after Christmas and Lady Day, the Monday in Whitsun week and the first Monday after Michaelmas Day. Rigid rules laid down the procedures of the club and members received payments for various accidents and discomfitures, *viz* a guinea for breaking a bone, five shillings per week for three months, then four shillings per week for the next three months, and two shillings for the next six months if he be inflicted with any disorder except what is listed in the seventh Article (venereal disease, injuries from unlawful quarrelling, wrestling, etc.). If her husband had been a member for three years, a new widow received eight pounds, towards which every member contributed a shilling with the rest coming from funds. Each member paid three shillings per quarter and could be fined for various offences, including sixpence for paying the quarterly fee late, sixpence for not being quiet after a meeting had been called to order, and two shillings and sixpence if guilty of profane swearing or striking a member in the Society's room.

The East Devon Hunt at Colaton Raleigh, *c.* 1949.

William Vowden, who worked at Hawkerland Farm before the First World War. His home was halfway between the Halfway House and the Cat and Fiddle at White Cross on the main Exeter road.

Colaton Raleigh, *c.* 1939.

Colaton Raleigh Methodist Chapel Sunday School anniversary, *c.* 1956. Back row, left to right: Mr Haysom, Mrs Haysom, Rosemary Taylor, Maureen Haysom, Revd C. Smith, Leonard Haysom. Front row: Linda Halpin, Evelyn Morris, Daphne Williams, Alan Halpin, Christine Williams, Helen Darch, Marion Halpin, Alec Kingdon, Adrian Haysom.

The coronation arch that took first prize at Colaton Raleigh in 1953.

A decorated arch celebrating the coronation of King George VI in 1937. Left to right: Norman Sellek, John Sellek, Bert Skinner, Norman Skinner, Mr Stawbridge, Percy Morrish, Leonard Bickley, Ned Board, Frank Strawbridge, Albert Bolt, Ralph Sellek.

Colaton Raleigh, *c.* 1906.

Church Road, Colaton Raleigh, *c.* 1900. Warren Cottage on the left was pulled down and replaced by Canterbury Green Cottages. The open space behind it, known as Paradise, was in front of two out-of-sight houses which have since been replaced by old people's homes known as Eden Way. The Barley Mow pub stood on the right. Burnt down in 1885, the premises were never licensed again.

Colaton Raleigh, *c.* 1910.

Hawkerland Farm, Colaton Raleigh, *c.* 1898. Samuel Sage, pictured here with his wife Maria and daughter Emily, never learnt to write his name and always signed his cheques with a cross.

Alberta Louisa Caroline Sage at Hawkerland Farm at the age of 19. Her niece Ethel Mary Bolt is visiting from Exeter.

Colaton Raleigh School, 1889. Alberta Louisa Caroline Bolt is the first pupil on the right of the second row from the back.

Sidmouth Road, Colaton Raleigh, *c.* 1920.

Sir Walter Raleigh's house, Colaton Raleigh, *c.* 1914.

Drupes Farm, Colaton Raleigh, *c.* 1918.

COLATON RALEIGH 28223

Colaton Raleigh, *c.* 1950.

Mr John Lugg at Selwood Farm, Colaton Raleigh, in around 1889.

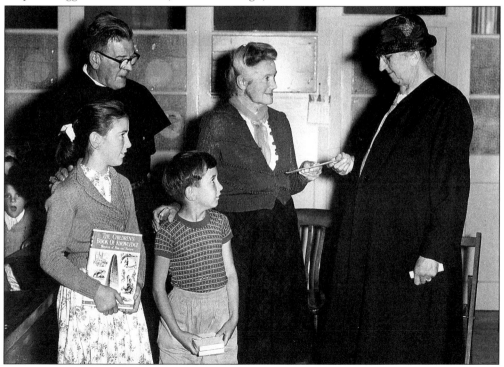

Mrs Greenslade retired as teacher at Colaton Raleigh in the mid-1950s when the school closed. She is seen here receiving a gift. Either side of her are Revd Piggot and Mrs Hettie Elliott. The children are Marion and Alan Halpin.

William Lugg watches his ploughman John Hitt in the fields at Selwood Farm, Colaton Raleigh, in the 1890s.

The Sage family at Warren Cottage near Woodbury in around 1905. Left to right are Reginald Charles Frank, who owed his three names to the fact that his mother wanted him called Reginald, his father Charles and his grandfather Frank, Matthew Samuel Sage, Rough the dog, Alberta Louisa Caroline Sage, named after Queen Caroline Louisa Alberta, and Nellie Florence Sage, named after Florence Nightingale.

William Lugg and one of his workmen crushing mangolds at Selwood Farm in around 1895.

The Otter Inn, Colaton Raleigh, c. 1935. Today the field on the right with the cow peacefully grazing is a children's playground.

Newton Poppleford, c. 1903.

Newton Poppleford in 1956, looking away from the village towards the River Otter. The Saxons, and before them the Romans, crossed the river at this spot via a ford. It was particularly stony, and 'pobble' being the Saxon word for stone (still used in some parts of Devon) the place not unnaturally became known as the 'pobble ford'. The 'new' and the 'ton' were added in the thirteenth century and probably refer to a newer settlement in the area.

Newton Poppleford in 1966.

Newton Poppleford, 1953. The Turks Head Inn stuck out into the road on a particularly dangerous bend where the then A35 main road entered the village on its way to Exeter; it later vanished in the interests of road safety. In more recent years the 30 m.p.h. signs have moved to the foot of Four Elms Hill and a rash of hideous red and yellow road signs and bumps have made an appearance.

Newton Poppleford in 1967.

The old Toll House, Newton Poppleford, 1961. Then an antiques shop but now up for sale, this is thought to have been Devon's only thatched toll house.

Newton Poppleford, *c.* 1931.

Preparing to leave from outside St Luke's church at the turn of the century. St Luke's was once a chantry church of the church of the Blessed Virgin Mary at Aylesbeare but was separated in 1862.

Harpford, c. 1908.

Harpford House, c. 1904. Left to right: Charlie Yates (with Bobs), Emily Peppin, her niece Gladys, Jack the dog, and Grandma Peppin.

124

Pump Cottage, Harpford, c. 1890. The unknown tenants are around the doorway. The ladies around the pump are the Peppin sisters, Katey, Lydia and Emily, from Harpford House.

Harpford, *c.* 1904.

Harpford House, *c.* 1890. Mrs Peppin is standing in the doorway with her daughter Lydia on her right; George Peppin is on the left with the dog, and Henry Peppin is second from right in the front.

St Gregory's church, Harpford, seen from Peakes garden, *c.* 1900. The Revd Augustus Toplady was vicar from 1766 to 1768 and there is a cross in the churchyard restored in his memory. The inscription on the cross includes a quotation from his hymn 'Rock of Ages', which was said to have been inspired by a visit to Burrington Combe in the Mendips during which he sheltered under a large rock in a particularly fierce storm.

Acknowledgments

We are indebted to Tony Gooding, both for his introduction and for allowing us full use of his magnificent collection of pictures of the Budleigh Salterton that he so obviously loves and serves as a fireman. Jim Perrian also kindly allowed us to use some of his family pictures, and Gerald Millington, Otterton's enthusiastic historian, provided many of the pictures of that lovely village. We thank all three.

Other pictures were lent by Joyce Atkinson, Bicton College of Agriculture (in particular the Principal's secretary Nicola O'Harry), Fergus Brown, Mr Caswill, Gilbert Cowd, Mrs D. Everest, Peggy Halpin, Mrs Harding, Mr B.N. Hawkes, Peggy Odam, Don Papworth, Dave Purdon and Budleigh Salterton Croquet Club, Ruth Roots, Doris Russell, Margaret Wheaton, Jerry and Janet Williams, Les Williams and East Budleigh AFC. We thank them all.

We would also like to thank our wives for their forbearance with our frequent absences, and the staff at Chalford Publishing, especially Simon Thraves, for putting up with us.